IDITAROD COUNTRY

Exploring the Route of The Last Great Race®

STORIES *by* TRICIA BROWN **PHOTOGRAPHY** *by* JEFF SCHULTZ

EPICENTER PRESS

Epicenter Press, Inc. is a regional press founded in Alaska whose interests include but are not limited to the arts, history, environment, and diverse cultures and lifestyles of the North Pacific and high latitudes. We seek both the traditional and innovative in publishing quality nonfiction tradebooks, contemporary art and photography giftbooks, and destination travel guides emphasizing Alaska, Washington, Oregon, and California.

PHOTOGRAPHS.

Front Cover: Shawn Sidelinger approaches Nome. Inset photos, from left: Tom Dotomain of Shaktoolik; a weary runner; a future musher in Kaltag; a Unalakleet mother and her baby.
Page 1: John Baker slips through a snow fence along the coast.
Page 3: Mushers pass a beached fishing boat outside Shaktoolik.
Page 7: Lending a hand in Nulato.
Page 8: Knik resident Tracy Thomas checks in musher John Gourley at Iditarod.

The Iditarod Trail Committee® holds registered trademarks for the following terms and language: Iditarod®, Iditarod Trail Committee®, Iditarod Trail Alaska®, Alaska where men are men and women win the Iditarod®, The Last Great Race®, 1,049 miles®, Anchorage to Nome®, and Mushing the Iditarod Trail®.

Editor: Christine Ummel
Photo Editor: Jeff Schultz
Cover and inside design: Elizabeth Watson
Proofreader: Lois Kelly
Map: Chris Arend Photography with art production
    by Penny Panlener
Base map © 1995 Hubbard Scientific, Division of
    American Education Products, used with permission.
Text © 1998 by Tricia Brown
Photos © 1998 by Jeff Schultz

Library of Congress Catalog Card Number: 97-077237
ISBN 0-945397-66-6

To order single copies of Iditarod Country, send $16.95 (Washington residents add $1.46 state sales tax) plus $5 for priority mail shipping to: Epicenter Press, Box 82368, Kenmore, WA 98028.

Booksellers: Retail discounts are available from our trade distributor, Graphic Arts Center Publishing™, Portland, Oregon; phone 800-452-3032.

Printed by Samhwa Printing Co., Ltd., Seoul, Korea.
First printing, February 1998
10 9 8 7 6 5 4 3 2

Contents

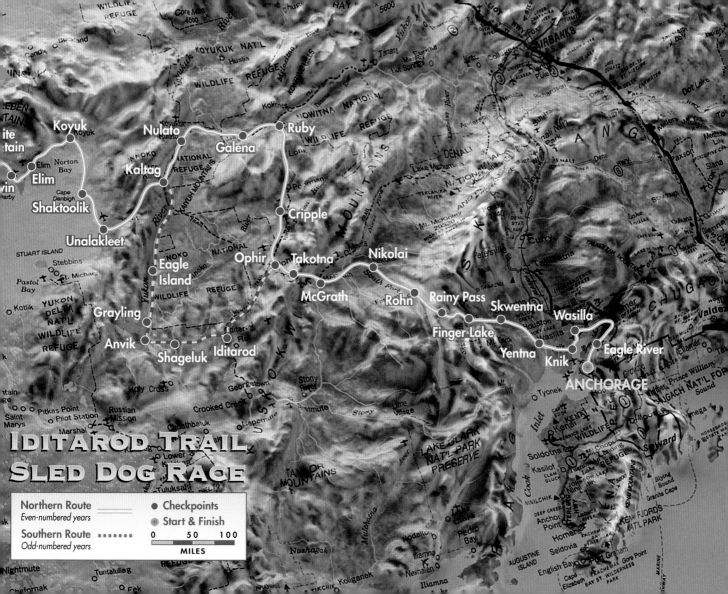

IDITAROD TRAIL SLED DOG RACE

Northern Route
Even-numbered years

Southern Route
Odd-numbered years

● Checkpoints
◉ Start & Finish

0   50   100
MILES

The Iditarod Family

Not so long ago, when people regularly traveled the Iditarod Trail by dog team, they found safe haven for themselves and their dogs at roadhouses in the villages along the way. And such it is today during the annual Iditarod Trail Sled Dog Race. Most of the checkpoints are in the same villages where mushers traditionally have stopped.

The Iditarod has evolved into a successful sporting event of international status in part because of the people who live in these communities along the trail. Can you imagine dozens of mushers coming into your town each winter for two weeks, spreading straw on the ground, and parking their teams in front of your city hall? They'd traipse in and out of the hall with pails of water and dog food. They'd hang their smelly, dirty, wet clothing over the heater. They'd nap on the floor, in the street, anywhere they wanted. The dogs would leave behind piles of feces and yellow snow; their unfinished food would be left to freeze on the ground.

And you'd volunteer to be up all hours of the night checking in these teams, telling them where to park, where to find water. Afterward you'd clean up their straw, dog feces, and frozen food. All simply to be a part of it.

It probably couldn't happen in many places, not for long anyway. But in Alaska, it's been going on since 1973. By now the Iditarod is so well-loved that more Alaskans know who won last year's Iditarod than who won last year's Super Bowl.

I've been an official Iditarod photographer since 1981, shuffling up and down the 1,100-mile trail in small planes and on snowmachines, going without sleep, and eating on the run for two weeks each March. And yet I keep coming back. There are three reasons.

First, the people. Behind the scenes are the down-to-earth "real" people who sacrifice their time and often their money for the Iditarod. Every year countless villagers help make the race happen by being there and pitching in. Though I usually see my Iditarod family only once a year, it's great to be a member.

Second, I enjoy the outdoors and the premise of the Iditarod, which pits mushers and dogs against Nature.

My third reason for coming back: I simply love it.

I hope you enjoy reading *Iditarod Country* and getting to know the Iditarod family. You're welcome to join us.

—*Jeff Schultz*

Introduction: The Heart of the Iditarod

For a thousand miles, the Iditarod Trail Sled Dog Race winds across Bush Alaska, a thinly populated, wild region that's inaccessible by road. On their journey, mushers pass through tall forests, cross mountain ranges, and venture onto the tundra. They travel along rivers and across frozen sea ice. To city folks, it might well seem another planet.

Waiting to greet the teams at the checkpoints—the connect-the-dots stopping places along the route—are volunteers who live in the Bush year-round or travel out just during racetime. Some Iditarod checkpoints are roadhouses or lodges that have been battened down for the winter, or a single cabin still standing in an abandoned gold-mining town. In a village, the checkpoint may be the community center, or perhaps a private residence. Most of these villages have fewer than three hundred residents. Many have a wash house for showers and laundry, one store, one school. Athabascan Indians, Inupiat Eskimos, and non-Natives alike count on fish and game as a mainstay of their diets.

Few Bush residents are wealthy, yet they are lavishly generous as they host a parade of old and new friends each March. They share their homes and food; cook for an army; haul supplies; and sacrifice time and sleep. (So that the same villages wouldn't bear this responsibility every year, a southern race route was added in 1977. The northern and southern routes, through different Athabascan villages, are used in alternating years.) Volunteers from Alaska's big cities and scores of people from around the country also fly in to join the trailside volunteers, often giving up their vacation time to sit in a cold tent with a clipboard, or flip pancakes, or shovel dog dirt.

Each year Race Manager Jack Niggemyer mobilizes an army of a thousand volunteers. He asks them to groom and mark the trail. He makes sure each checkpoint has a parking area for dogs, a check-in person, a race judge, a veterinarian, and a clean-up crew. He also sees that seventy-five tons of dog food, straw, and musher supplies are flown into the checkpoints by the volunteer pilots of the "Iditarod Air Force."

Once the freight hits the runway, it's up to the locals to move it to the village's staging area. They also secure a place for mushers and visiting volunteers to sleep. Each checkpoint needs access to water and coordinated air transportation for race officials and dropped dogs. Communications must be in place.

Since the Iditarod's first running in 1973, there have been many changes in the race, from new rules, to upgrades in outdoor fabrics and mushing gear, to advancements in communications. And yet many of the same faces and names have stayed involved in the race since its beginning. In this book, you'll only meet a handful of them. We wish we had room for more.

—*Tricia Brown*

ANCHORAGE

POPULATION: 254,000

◀ ◀ **Thousands of spectators line the sidewalks along Anchorage's Fourth Avenue on race day.**

▶ **With cameras recording his every move, Charlie Boulding checks his team one last time before boarding his sled on the starting line.**

The Iditarod makes a date with Anchorage for the first Saturday of every March, and with it comes a circus for the senses.

Snow-removal equipment operators work through Friday night in a weird change of mission. Instead of plowing the snow away, they dump tons of it onto a downtown street. Temporary fencing is installed along both sides of Fourth Avenue for many blocks. On Saturday morning there's barely room for a single file of bodies to pass through the fans stacked along the sidewalks. Coffee and hot chocolate sales are brisk, and youngsters are hawking race programs. It's bright and cold.

Over loudspeakers, sportscasters chat about statistics, weather, and winning strategies. Their voices are the bass line in the symphony of the starting line. Above it hangs a ragged melody of keening and barking from dog teams "parked" in the staging areas. Most are Iditarod veterans, and they're ready to run.

Mushers wear numbered bibs over heavy winter clothing that swishes as they walk around their dog trucks, murmuring to their dogs, checking gear, pausing to greet friends or pose for photos.

The attention of the crowd—fans, volunteers, photographers, television cameramen, and filmmakers—is focused on the starting line beneath a fancy banner. Every two minutes, a team advances to the line, dogs straining against their handlers, the musher riding the brake. Stopped on the mark, with handlers gripping their harnesses, a few dogs look back as if to ask, "What's the hold-up? Let's go."

The announcer begins the countdown from ten, and the musher, who's been assuring the team with touches and encouraging words, pats the leaders once more, then lopes back to the sled. At "three-two-ONE!" the dogs, like unbound springs, lunge forward.

Away they run down a corridor between storefronts and packed sidewalks, amid shouts of encouragement, crystallized breath, and the thudding applause of mitted hands. Taking long, powerful strides, the dogs seem to fly along the main street of Alaska's biggest city, where half the state's population lives, and where—as in the Iditarod itself—the civilized and the wild have made an uneasy alliance. Running on instinct and desire, they begin the 1,100-mile journey to Nome.

EAGLE RIVER

POPULATION: 28,600

MILES FROM ANCHORAGE: 20

▲ Race Manager Jack Niggemyer says he packs a machete on board his snowmachine to keep his volunteers in line. Actually, Niggemyer uses the blade to brush trail.

▶ Between Anchorage and Eagle River, drivers on the Glenn Highway get a close-up view of the race.

Pockets of Iditarod fans station themselves along the "urban trail" between Anchorage and the nearby town of Eagle River. Even drivers on the four-lane Glenn Highway can follow the action from their car windows as northbound mushers edge around the foothills of the Chugach Range.

"Traveling along the trail is fun, just even going out of Anchorage," says Race Manager Jack Niggemyer. "A couple of years ago, I rode on my friend's second sled for the start of the Iditarod, and I was astounded at the number of people partying along the trail. Our sled was half-full of junk by the time we got to Eagle River: muffins and coffee and beer and cheeseburgers . . .

"My friend was Bert Hanson, and everybody was yelling, 'Go, Bert, go!' And I thought, 'God, he knows everybody in this town,' until I realized that they all had their programs and were looking up his bib number."

At Eagle River, the mushers are met by members of their support crews. Teams are unharnessed and loaded into dog trucks for the drive to the next stop, thus avoiding open water on the Knik River and the often-snowless area called the Palmer Flats.

WASILLA

(*wah*-SILL-*a*)

POPULATION: 4,714

MILES FROM EAGLE RIVER: 29

▼ **Jerry Austin heads down the Wasilla runway in the Restart, one day after the ceremonial beginning in Anchorage.**

On Sunday morning, the mushers queue up again for what's called the Restart. The official clock starts ticking when they leave the starting line on the old Wasilla runway. The broad sky and open spaces of the Matanuska-Susitna Valley are a stark contrast to Anchorage's crowded Fourth Avenue start as the mushers head across Wasilla Lake to Lake Lucille. Traveling along the edge of Knik-

Goose Bay Road, the teams follow a trail frequently used by valley snowmachiners. Locals haul barbecue grills and lawn chairs to the ends of their driveways, forming mini-cheering squads that are so close to the trail they can offer passing mushers a "low five." At these parties, ice chests are used not to chill the beer and sodas, but to keep the drinks from freezing.

KNIK

(*kuh*-NIK)

POPULATION: 445

MILES FROM WASILLA: 14

◀ Sven Engholm's dogs charge forward, eager to begin their run to Nome.

▲ Dan and Pat Eckert wave to musher Malcom Vance from their comfortable trailside seating.

▶ Knik is the last place along the Iditarod Trail that's still accessible via the road system.

On their way to Knik, teams pass a massive log building that houses the Iditarod headquarters and museum. Inside, among the artifacts, is the stuffed and mounted body of Togo, one of the famed lead dogs instrumental in delivering life-saving diphtheria serum to Nome in 1925.

Knik, where the Mushers Hall of Fame is located, also is home to many notable mushers, among them the "Father of the Iditarod" Joe Redington Sr., who founded the Iditarod in 1973. At age eighty, Redington competed in the race's twenty-fifth anniversary running in 1997. From Knik, the mushers leave the road system for good.

YENTNA

(YENT-*na*)

POPULATION: 8

MILES FROM KNIK: 52

◄ ◄ An aerial view of Skwentna. Skwentna isn't a town proper, but rather a community that's spread over several miles along the river.
▼ Winter and summer, the Yentna Station Roadhouse is one of the busiest spots on the river.

You'd think life in a remote wilderness lodge would offer a little peace and quiet. That's not the case for the Gabryszak family, who operate the Yentna Station Roadhouse on a switchback of the Yentna River called the Big Bend.

"We're on a snowmachine trail. It's like a highway out there with just regular business going by," says Jean Gabryszak. "We sell gas, and we have rooms and food. In summers, we get a lot of fishermen, and we do charters. In winters, a lot of the mushers train out there, too."

Jean and her husband Dan had one daughter when they moved up from Reno and built the place back in 1977. Since then, they've added five more children, all of whom are home-schooled by their mother.

"We do school all year round because some days in the winter, it's just non-stop traffic. Several weeks we don't get anything done, then we work at it hard again. From January through March, it's just do it when you can."

You might say the Gabryszaks are professional checkpoint people. Jean remembers the year that, besides the Iditarod, they served as a checkpoint for the Knik 200 sled dog race, the Klondike 300 sled dog race, the Klondike 400 snowmachine race, the Iditasport, the Junior Iditarod, and the Iron Dog.

For the Iditarod, Jean and her helpers offer free spaghetti dinners to the mushers in exchange for their autographs on posters that go to the volunteers.

SKWENTNA

(SKWENT-*na*)

POPULATION: 86

MILES FROM YENTNA: 34

▼ **Skwentna can cook. Residents along the river pitch in to serve a memorable feast to mushers, officials, and journalists.**

As mushers near the confluence of the Yentna and Skwentna Rivers, they look for the signs to Norma and Joe Delia's log cabin, eager to check in, tend their dogs, and get inside. They know that the "Skwentna Sweeties," an army of two dozen local volunteers led by Norma, have cooked up a dinner matched only by Mom's Thanksgiving menu. Besides the main dish—roast turkey one night, roast beef the next—there's dressing, potatoes, gravy, coleslaw, yams, homemade rolls, pickles, and olives.

The couple's hospitality is legendary; the thousands of meals they've served over the years have been paid for out of pocket. When the guest list grows to nearly four hundred people in the space of a few days, as it did one year, meals are constantly standing room only. The floor of the Delias' two-story cabin measures twenty-four by thirty-two feet.

Joe Delia, who's been Skwentna's postmaster for twenty years, has volunteered for the Iditarod since the beginning. As Norma tells it, more than twenty-five years ago, Joe was out checking his trapline when suddenly a man skied out of the woods.

"It startled both of them," Norma says. "The guy said he was scouting the Iditarod Trail." Next, race founder Joe Redington Sr. and musher Dick Mackey flew out for a visit.

"Joe showed them through his trapline. It was the only thing going through at that time." With that, Delia's trapline was incorporated into the cross-country race. "We always tease and say we have a national trapline," says Norma.

21

FINGER LAKE

POPULATION: 2

MILES FROM SKWENTNA: 45

◀◀ **Vern Halter and team cross Puntilla Lake at Rainy Pass.**

▼ **Joe Redington Sr. arrives at the Finger Lake checkpoint.**

Veteran mushers fondly remember former Finger Lake residents Gene and June Leonard, who were active Iditarod supporters for almost twenty years. Their cabin was a checkpoint when the race first came through in 1973, and Gene was inspired to run it himself. He did so four times, finishing twice.

More recently, volunteers Kirsten and Barry Stanley held down the Finger Lake post. At the base of the Alaska Range, in the midst of the timber, the checkpoint lodge is perfectly situated for snow lovers. One weather system after another can dump as many as ten feet of snow.

"The front porch in the summer was three steps down," Kirsten remembers. "In the winter, it was three to six steps up to get out of the hole."

Kirsten was raised in Knik, where she and her brother cared for sixty dogs and competed in the Junior Iditarod. Kirsten did well, but decided against stepping up to the Iditarod.

"I started running dogs at age nine. By eighteen I'd had enough," she says.

Kirsten and Barry worked at Finger Lake for three years before passing on the job to their replacements. Now based in Willow, Barry flies out for a few days every summer to help brush out the Iditarod Trail. For the last twelve years, he's been responsible for putting in the trail between Finger Lake and Rohn.

"A lot of the mushers will tell you that's the worst stretch of trail," says Kirsten. That's not to speak poorly of Barry's work. The terrain is steep and treacherous, winding through heavy timber and sidehills, what Race Manager Jack Niggemyer calls "the hairiest part of the trail."

RAINY PASS

POPULATION: 2

MILES FROM FINGER LAKE: 30

▲ Frank Karash and Cathy Peterson are volunteers at the Rainy Pass checkpoint.

▶ At 1,800 feet elevation, the lodge at Rainy Pass is several miles below the actual pass.

Before and after their stint at Finger Lake, Kirsten and Barry Stanley spent more than eight years as roadhouse caretakers at the Rainy Pass Lodge on Puntilla Lake. They were the only wintertime residents, but they weren't alone.

"Actually when you live out there, you have more company than when you live in town," Kirsten says. "Snowmachiners can get there really easy. A lot of airplanes on bad weather days—planes can't get through, so they land and come in for coffee and cookies."

The lodge on Puntilla Lake is at 1,800 feet, right at timberline. When mushers leave the checkpoint, they travel uphill for miles to Rainy Pass itself, where they cross the highest point on the trail at 3,160 feet. Whiteout conditions can occur. "From scary to scarier" best describes the trail over the top. Waiting on the other side is Dalzell Gorge, which Jack Niggemyer describes as "probably the most singularly terrifying thing on the whole race. Or it can be, depending on the weather.

"You're going downhill at the bottom of a narrow canyon, winding back and forth across the creek, so you've got a lot of sidehills and open water. And big holes in the ice. And rocks you can't move. Once you get down to the bottom, where it drains into the Tatina River, and you've gotta run across there for a couple of miles, overflow is common. We can go put the trail in, and two hours later, there's icy slush, and two hours after that, it can be bare ground."

ROHN

(RONE)

POPULATION: 0

MILES FROM RAINY PASS: 48

▲ Television film crews interview veterinarian Al Townsend.

▶ The Rohn posse, among them the Mayor and the Sheriff. From left, Rudi Indermuhl, Denny Plano, Eric Rogers, Bill Brown, Dave Oleson, and Terry Boyle. Crouching: Jasper Bond.

▶▶ Raymie Redington negotiates a section of rough trail about thirteen miles out of Rohn.

For a few weeks of every year, an Alaskan and a Minnesotan are the Mayor and the Sheriff of Rohn. The two men, Terry Boyle and Jasper Bond, have been stationed at the Rohn checkpoint—which consists of a lone cabin near the confluence of the Kuskokwim River's South Fork and the Tatina River—since the early '90s. Who's mayor and who's sheriff? Who knows. Maybe they switch every year. But one thing is certain: They've got the best assignment. Most people consider Rohn the most scenic checkpoint on the trail.

A roadhouse once stood here to serve the dog-mushing mail carriers and other travelers on the original Iditarod Trail. That building is gone now, but in its place stands the cabin, which was constructed in the 1930s and is listed on the National Register of Historic Places. Unlike most of the checkpoint buildings, which are privately owned, the cabin is managed by the Bureau of Land Management, which strictly limits its use.

From the beauty of Rohn, mushers head into some of the most difficult stretches of trail, leaving the Alaska Range through what are known as the Buffalo Tunnels. "That's some fairly steep timber there where the buffalo like to hang out. They're what basically keep the trail open," says Jack Niggemyer.

About twenty miles below Rohn, the mushers arrive at the infamous Farewell Burn. In 1977, thousands of acres burned in the Bear Creek fire, and the resulting deadfall, coupled with low snowfall, makes for a bumpy, sled-shredding ride.

NIKOLAI

(NIK-*o-lye*)

POPULATION: 109

MILES FROM ROHN: 93

◄◄ **Simon Kinneen pulls into Nikolai.**

▼ **Local children Cheryl Graham and Joseph Stokes share their schoolyard with resting Iditarod dogs.**

Nikolai is a pretty little village of log cabins and frame houses nestled among the trees. Its centerpiece is a lovely Russian Orthodox church, built in the late 1920s, with its three onion-shaped domes topped by crosses. From Nikolai, there's an unsurpassed view of the back side of Mount McKinley, just a hundred miles to the west.

This is the first of the Alaska Native villages that the mushers pass through in the race. Almost everyone here is Athabascan Indian, a group that once claimed all of Interior Alaska and parts of Southcentral.

"We're about 90 percent Athabascan, and there's two guys from Minnesota and one from Wisconsin," jokes City Manager Roger Jenkins, one of the two former Minnesotans.

Nikolai has a restaurant and a lodge, and during the Iditarod the local kids open their own restaurant. Check-in volunteers are chosen by drawing names out of a hat.

Radio volunteers and the race veterinarian are set up in the city building, which serves as the checkpoint. Mushers who take their twenty-four-hour break here are welcomed into the shop, a forty-by-sixty building that's toasty warm on the coldest nights.

Jenkins still remembers the year Rick Swenson came into Nikolai when the thermometer was hanging at fifty below zero.

"One of the locals, Ignaty Petruska, was standing here, and Rick asked him, 'Ignaty, how cold does it have to be before you put your earflaps down?'

"It was just a beautiful question. Ignaty didn't have to say anything. It wasn't cold enough to put 'em down."

McGRATH

POPULATION: 466

MILES FROM NIKOLAI: 48

▲ **A lonely traveler checks out his surroundings. Today he'll be loaded onto a plane with other tired or sick dogs who are headed home.**

▶ **Dropped dogs are transferred first to McGrath by small plane. From there, they travel by jet to Anchorage.**

At the confluence of the Kuskokwim and Takotna Rivers, McGrath may not be accessible by road, but it's a regional hub with stores, restaurants, a bar or two, and a full-service airport. During the race, air traffic creates a constant buzz. Tired or sick dogs are flown here from other checkpoints to await transport back to Anchorage.

Here, too, is a central communications point, and the place where many mushers take their twenty-four-hour layover. And the first musher to hit town receives the Golden Pace Award: a gold nugget watch from the Alaska Commercial Company.

Managing the race, Jack Niggemyer makes McGrath his mini-headquarters for a few days.

"It's kind of chaos," Niggemyer says. His regular helpers include checker Mark Cox and former Iditarod musher Eep Anderson.

"The first half of the race it's always interesting to watch the mushers dice out their twenty-four-hour layover," Niggemyer says. "You don't really know who's in first place until they're all done with it. Generally somewhere between Nikolai and Takotna and Ophir is where most take it—on that one little seventy-five-mile stretch of trail.

"You've got teams roaring through McGrath, still heading up the trail, and you've got other guys sitting halfway through their twenty-four-hour layover back in Nikolai. So it seems a lot of time is spent by the locals, and by all of us, sitting there looking at the sheets to see who really is in first place. Somebody could be the first team to Ophir, but realistically be in fifteenth place.

"They've kinda gotten over the first day or two jitters of getting out on the trail, they've gotten over that big obstacle, the Alaska Range, the Farewell Burn, now it's time to start dicing out—see who's racing, see who's camping."

TAKOTNA

(*ta*-COT-*na*)

POPULATION: 46

MILES FROM MCGRATH: 23

▲ Takotna is famous for over-stuffing mushers.

▶ Schoolchildren tend the fire, making hot water available for mushers who need it to prepare dog food.

▶▶ In a streak of creativity, local kids sculpted their own dog team out of snow.

Above the banks of the Takotna River, set amid the spruce and birch, this village is an important refueling stop for mushers, thanks to the efforts of Dick and Jan Newton and before them, Eep and Pudden Anderson.

"You can't eat enough there," says one Iditarod official, remembering the sumptuous meals he's enjoyed over the years.

Mushers, pilots, and journalists are fed like kings with stacks of hot cakes, breakfast meats, burgers, crab, steak, turkey, and the longtime favorites that are always on the stove: moose stew and chili.

"Anything to make them feel at home," says Jan Newton, who was initiated into the Iditarod

when she and Dick moved to Takotna in 1976. Back then, Anderson was competing in the race while his wife held down the checkpoint.

"Pudden's the one that got me involved," Jan says. "She told me, 'Oh, you'll have lots of fun, meet new people.'" When the Andersons moved to McGrath, the Newtons took over. And once Takotna's new community building opened, offering more room for hospitality, more residents got behind the race, donating food and offering to cook meals.

When the pre-race planes arrive with supplies, Dick calls the village school. The teenagers are let out of class to jump on their snowmachines and help him haul the goods to storage. Closer to race time, they move the supplies—dog food, stove fuel, straw, pails, disposable dishes, and more—to the checkpoint and alphabetize them to make it easier for tired mushers to find their shipments.

"We've had mushers come in that were so tired they basically didn't know where they were," Jan says. "They only want to rest a half-hour. You try to wake them up and ask, 'Are you awake?' 'Yes.' And then you come back and they're asleep again and they sleep for the next six or eight hours."

OPHIR

(OH-*fur*)

POPULATION: 0

MILES FROM TAKOTNA: 38

◀ From Takotna, the Iditarod Trail leads northwest through gold-mining country to Ophir.

▼ Dave Sawatzky arrives in Ophir, a ghost town in an old mining district.

The 1908 discovery of gold near Ophir put this place on the map with a biblical name referring to the source of King Solomon's gold. However, Ophir soon faded into a ghost town. Today just one cabin stands, owned by Dick and Audra Forsgren, who devoted themselves to volunteering when Ophir became an official checkpoint in 1974.

Working with the Forsgrens was a local gold-miner, a man that many know simply as "The Loafer from Ophir."

"If I did nothing but mining, I'd make a living at it, but it got boring. That's why I joined the Iditarod. I got bored," says the Loafer, whose

real name is Roger Roberts. How'd he come by his nickname? Here's his story about what happened during one summer mining season:

"When I first went out to Ophir I was prospecting in the hills, and I had a hundred dogs parked in the valley. I would backpack all I could carry and go up in the mountains, prospecting. I'd work around the clock, 'cause the sun don't go down. Fourteen, sixteen, eighteen hours. Then I'd backpack down, feed the dogs, and go to bed. Didn't matter what time it was.

"Invariably, I'd lay down in the afternoon to sleep, and these guys who'd come by from the Public Health Service, getting paid by the hour, started calling me a loafer. I'd say, 'If you believe I'm a loafer, I'd like you to try and keep up with me for a half day.'"

True to his word, the Loafer pitches in with the best of them for the Iditarod.

"If bridges need building, I build bridges. If they need somebody to break trail, I break trail. I haul dog food, take care of sick dogs, whatever needs doing."

From Ophir, the race route splits. On even-numbered years, it follows the northern route to Cripple. For odd-numbered years, the trail heads south to Iditarod.

CRIPPLE

POPULATION: 0

MILES FROM OPHIR: 60

▲ Joe Redington Sr., an old fox who proved he still had a few tricks up his sleeve.

▶ Doug Swingley arrives at the Cripple checkpoint tent. Like Ophir and Iditarod, Cripple was once a bustling gold-mining supply town. Today there's nary a soul to call it home.

The Cripple checkpoint is not for the faint of heart—it's merely a tent on the Innoko River near the broken-down remains of what was a small settlement. The temperature can range from ten to fifty-five. That's below zero. Nevertheless, Dick Westlund is faithfully waiting to shake the hand of the first musher there, ready to present the GCI Dorothy G. Page Halfway Award of $3,000 in gold nuggets.

Jules and Leslie Mead hosted the checkpoint from 1978 to 1984 when a small, T-shaped cabin was still standing. As operators of Teeland's Country Store in Wasilla, they were often asked to support individual mushers, so they decided to do something for all of them: feed them first-class meals at no charge from the cabin at Cripple.

Jules remembers those early days of the Iditarod, when the pace was much slower. Mushers took more time at the checkpoints to kick back and share a few stories, even while they kept a wary eye on each other.

"In our first year, 1978, all of the mushers had taken their twenty-four-hour layover at McGrath or sooner," Jules says. "When they got to Cripple, we had about fifteen of them in that afternoon and into the evening. We fed them, wined them and dined them. They actually had a party that night. The next morning they were all sitting around the breakfast table and talking about taking another twenty-four hours. They'd agreed that it would be no problem if everybody stayed put.

"We were kind of getting near the end of breakfast time and Joe Redington snuck out. When they saw him flying by the window, everybody jumped up and started scrambling."

Although that small cabin is now gone, Iditarod fans well remember the thrilling climax of that 1978 race, when Dick Mackey beat Rick Swenson by the nose of his lead dog—a split-second victory that might have turned out otherwise if not for that leisurely breakfast at Cripple.

RUBY

POPULATION: 190

MILES FROM CRIPPLE: 112

▼ John Cooper leaves Ruby, a village that's built in tiers above the Yukon River.

Another prize awaits the first musher to reach Ruby: a seven-course gourmet meal prepared by a chef from Anchorage's Regal Alaskan hotel. With the dinner comes $3,500 in cash for the First Musher to the Yukon Award.

Ruby's streets are tiered back into a little bowl along the Yukon River at its junction with the Melozitna River. Most homes are log cabins, but fifteen brand-new frame houses were recently finished. The village was originally established by a minor gold rush around 1911,

and within a few years, its population boomed to more than a thousand. Since the 1920s, fewer than two hundred people, mostly Athabascans, have lived here year-round.

Postmaster Ron Inlow oversees the checkpoint's team of about a dozen local volunteers, who are joined by fly-in volunteers from as far away as Australia and Scandinavia.

"I usually put up notices a month ahead and try to get all the ladies going. We have a big, continuous smorgasbord for all the mushers and volunteers." The fare includes local favorites such as moose head soup, Native ice cream, moose stew, or fish stew.

When the racers have passed through Ruby, leftover dog food is donated to local sprint mushers who compete in spring carnivals held in villages along the river. As for Inlow, he claims the piles of used straw. He's one of Interior Alaska's hardy breed of vegetable gardeners. Never mind that a hard frost visits Ruby by the third week of August.

"I dump the straw at the end of my garden. In spring, I'll rototill it in," he says. "I grow mostly root vegetables: potatoes, carrots, broccoli, turnips. We even got some corn this year. We got six ears of corn."

GALENA
*(guh-*LEEN-*uh)*

POPULATION: 529

MILES FROM RUBY: 52

▼ With help from a volunteer handler, Rick Mackey is directed to the area where his team can rest.

Not only did Galena supply the Iditarod with 1974 champion Carl Huntington, it is also home to a state treasure: Edgar Nollner, the last living participant of the 1925 diphtheria serum run. This historic event remains an important symbol of the selfless spirit of Alaska's villages. From Nenana to Nome, the villages sent out a chain of mushers to pass along the serum that would halt the spreading epidemic. Nollner was then twenty-two.

"He never drank, never smoked, never even drank coffee," says Nollner's granddaughter, Rose Yaeger-Lund, who grew up to become a sprint musher herself. And from 1973 to 1990, Rose organized the Galena checkpoint for the Iditarod.

"It's like go-go-go for almost two weeks. I've always enjoyed it."

When Rose moved to Anchorage in 1990, she sold her sprint dogs to long-time friend Susan Butcher, who'd wanted to buy the dogs long before Rose was ready to sell.

"I had dogs from Huslia and Hughes and Ruby, and they've become the best dogs," Rose says with pride.

As for her grandfather, who's now in his nineties, Rose keeps an eye on him from Anchorage: "I'm going to try to get him down to the Iditarod start, even if I have to go up and bring him down.

"I just worry about him all the time. A couple winters ago I called him, and when he answered the phone he sounded out of breath. I said, 'What are you doing?' He was up shoveling snow on the roof! I said, 'God, Grandpa, you've got a hundred grandkids. You've got to get them to help you.'

"'Oh no, I like to do it myself.'"

NULATO

(*noo*-LA-*toh*)

POPULATION: 349

MILES FROM GALENA: 52

Founded in 1838 by Nalakov, "The Russian Creole," Nulato was once the site of many bloody killings as Europeans repeatedly tried to establish a trading post along the Yukon River. Attacks by the local Athabascans, it seemed, did not dissuade them. Although earlier buildings were raided and burned, a new fort and trading post were built in the mid-1850s. Contrary to popular belief, when Russia sold Alaska to the United States in 1867, the deal did not include any of the land, which the Russians had never claimed. Instead, they sold trading rights, docks, warehouses, and other buildings, including the Russian settlement at Nulato.

Today the Athabascans own Nulato, one of a few Native villages where dog mushing hasn't been abandoned for the convenience of snowmachines. According to long-time Iditarod checker Larry Esmailka, there are "plenty of dogs" and several mushers in Nulato. One man is planning to enter the Iditarod one day. Three others are sprint racers.

Esmailka is one of six local people who regularly volunteer for the Iditarod, marking the trail, hauling water for the dogs, waiting for mushers to check in.

"I'm looking forward to it," Esmailka says. "I like meeting the mushers, checking for mandatory gear, getting them in and out. A lot of people cook Native foods for them like moose meat, salmon, beaver meat, everything.

"After the Iditarod comes through, the carnivals kick in—spring carnivals all over. We go to other villages for dog races, snowshoe races, pretty good times, snowmachine races, everything like that.

"In March, it's about twenty to thirty below. The weather's pretty mild—starting to warm up."

► Volunteers of all ages pitch in to move dog food and supplies in Nulato.

KAL/TAG

(KAL-*tag*)

POPULATION: 232

MILES FROM EAGLE ISLAND

ON SOUTHERN ROUTE: 70

MILES FROM NULATO ON

NORTHERN ROUTE: 42

◄ DeeDee Jonrowe departs Nulato and heads for the trail to Kaltag.
► A Kaltag youngster pretends he's an Iditarod musher. While Athabascan villages on the northern and southern routes host the Iditarod in alternating years, Kaltag is a checkpoint every year. This is where the separate routes converge.

Kaltag is the last Athabascan Indian village before mushers cross an invisible boundary into Inupiat Eskimo country. From here, the trail leaves the Yukon River and heads into the Nulato Hills through Old Woman Pass to reach the Bering Sea.

"We're Athabascan, but a lot of the people originally came from a place called Whale Back between here and Unalakleet. Some of our dances and traditions have come from the trading a long time ago with the Eskimos," says Violet Burnham, a lifelong resident who's been a checkpoint worker since the early days of the Iditarod.

Violet's husband, Richard, is a transplant from Oregon. A musher in the 1975 Iditarod, Richard arrived in Kaltag, fell in love with the place, and immediately negotiated to buy a house. He ran the Iditarod four times, placing in the money twice, before he switched roles to checkpoint volunteer.

"Richard does most of the work because we have four kids," Violet says. "He and another guy, Philip Semaken, prepare the community hall by getting wood for the stove, bringing in some water barrels, sorting out the dog food as it comes in.

"Our house is used mainly for Iditarod personnel, photographers, veterinarians, the race judge or marshal. We live right on the banks of the river, so we usually can tell when mushers are coming.

"It's crazy for about a week."

IDITAROD

(*eye*-DID-*a-rod*)

POPULATION: 0

MILES FROM OPHIR: 90

◄◄ **Peryll Kyzer, Tim Osmar, and Vern Halter are within yards of each other as they travel on the frozen Yukon River.**

▲ **An old steam engine is among the remains of the old gold-mining town.**

► **The Iditadog hot dog stand did brisk business during its one-season opener.**

Rusted-out equipment and a little trapping cabin are all that stand where once there was a bustling mining hub of 10,000 people. Between 1908 and 1925, about $35 million in gold was taken from the region, back when gold was $20 an ounce.

Gold is moving through Iditarod a little differently now. To mark the halfway point on the southern route, GCI's Dick Westlund meets the first musher with a trophy and $3,000 in gold nuggets.

About fifteen miles away is Flat, home to a half-dozen people who one year decided they wanted to join the event. Iditarod pilot Reagan Russey remembers flying into Flat with the race manager about a month before the 1982 race. The men were making an early run to set up various checkpoints. At Flat, the villagers asked how they could be involved.

"I suggested, 'Why don't you set up a concession over at Iditarod?'" Reagan says. "I told them they'd be on national television. We talked about it very briefly."

During the race, when Reagan landed at Iditarod, he was surprised to see that the villagers had taken his advice.

"They'd gone all out—full blown," he says.

"They'd hauled barbecues out there and set up a big tent on a platform. They put up a sign that said, 'You Drop 'Em, We Chop 'Em.' Hot dogs and sodas. It was really elaborate, and it went over great."

Reagan is one of about two dozen members of the "Iditarod Air Force" who volunteer their time and private aircraft for the race, moving hundreds of people and seventy-five tons of supplies to checkpoints along the trail.

"Every year is different. I always go out in February and put the remote checkpoints in. Then I go back out during the race. Forty to fifty hours of flying time is normal for most of our pilots."

SHAGELUK

(SHAG-*a-luck*)

POPULATION: 139

MILES FROM IDITAROD: 65

▲ Leading mushers like Martin Buser rely on "power naps" to boost their energy levels in the last half of the race.

▶ Lavon Barve checks in at Shageluk, an Indian village on the Innoko River.

Snug along the banks of the Innoko River, Shageluk is an Athabascan Indian community whose name means "village of the dog people." Long-time volunteer Arnold Hamilton and his uncle Hamilton Hamilton, along with a few other adults and teenagers, are there to greet incoming mushers and direct them to the stash of dog food, straw, and water. Most Shageluk homes are log cabins; newer frame buildings include the school, the village store, and the "Washeteria," where everybody goes to take showers and do their laundry. In winter, men run traplines; in summer, the villagers depend on subsistence fishing. On clear March nights, it can still get down to twenty below zero.

One of Martin Buser's most memorable moments in Shageluk is one he doesn't even remember. But the people who told him about it, he says, are "reasonably reliable."

Exhausted and ready for a power nap, Martin had stretched out underneath the pool table in the community center.

"I put my little alarm clock in my hat—that way I get woken up and nobody can turn it off for me," he says. "The alarm went off and I tried to get up, but since I was under a table, I sat up and knocked myself out cold and went back to sleep. They say I repeated that procedure a couple of times. Then when I finally got on my feet, I walked into a wall when I was trying to shake the sleepies out of my eyes."

Somehow Buser finally found the door, and as the cold air cleared his head, he went about the business of leaving Shageluk.

"I never remembered a thing."

ANVIK

(ANN-*vick*)

POPULATION: 91

MILES FROM SHAGELUK: 25

▲ The view of the slough and downtown Anvik, the home of veteran Iditarod musher Ken Chase.

▶ The center of attention, Jeff King is seated for his award dinner.

During odd-numbered years, $3,500 in cash plus a fabulous meal—a seven-course gourmet spread prepared by a chef from Anchorage's Regal Alaskan hotel—is given to the first musher to reach Anvik. Here's how Iditarod Race Manager Jack Niggemyer recalls the year Jeff King arrived for "dinner" at 4 a.m.:

"I remember sitting in this little community hall, and that there were these distinct groups. First you had the musher—this wind-encrusted abomination coming out of the woods—Jeff, with his big, icy walrus mustache. He was real gracious; he wasn't going to stay long, but he had to eat his dinner.

"There were the locals, who were up, excited, and sitting somewhat quietly in the back of the room. Off to the side you had us hard-core race people, myself and a couple

pilots, and one or two veterinarians who were just kinda wishing we could be asleep—we'd seen this before.

"Then you had the guys from the Regal Alaskan wearing their tuxes and their bunny boots and their fur hats, and all this fancy crystalware, and they were doing their little show, which was wonderful.

"Then you had the press. These guys are all thinking they're going to have some kind of epiphany about the race by getting their camera right up and watching Jeff actually masticating his food. We're all shaking our heads.

"One of these guys has a television camera with a viewfinder that you look down in, and he's leaning over to get a picture. He's leaning over close to the candelabra, and suddenly he catches his hair on fire!

"Here you got this musher, and these guys in tuxedos, cooking, looking, and all the locals in the back, and us shaking our heads over here while this guy's running around beating his head with both hands.

"And I'm thinking, 'How am I ever going to explain this to anybody? How am I ever going to get across how bizarre and surreal this whole scene is?'"

GRAYLING

POPULATION: 203

MILES FROM ANVIK: 18

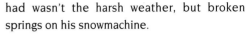

▼ **Long-time checker Joe Maillelle Sr. assists musher Mike Madden.**

Mushers agree that there are disadvantages to taking the southern route. One of them is traveling on the Yukon River with the wind in your face. Traveling on the northern route means it's at your back.

Grayling trailbreaker Carl Walker Jr. attests to the difference: "In March, the wind blows and it's always deep snow. It's not really too bad, but the winds come down the Yukon and can obliterate the trail five minutes after you go by."

Carl breaks trail on the river between Kaltag and Eagle Island. The worst trouble he's had wasn't the harsh weather, but broken springs on his snowmachine.

"Nothing drastic," he says. "Always somebody coming by anyway. When you make a trail, then everybody else comes by."

Before a 1992 rule change, mushers were allowed to stay in villagers' homes. The new "corralling rule" dictates that all mushers rest in the same sleeping area so officials can be assured that no musher is receiving illegal assistance, and veterinarians don't have to traipse all over the village looking for the teams that they're supposed to check. But the rule change was unpopular with villagers who looked forward to housing individual mushers.

Carl enjoyed putting up Rick Swenson, Susan Butcher, Sonny Lindner, and others. Even with the rule change, villagers like Carl still find ways to give.

"It's just natural—we do that—we've been that way for thousands of years, paid or not. Some guys lose an ax, I give 'em mine. We give people salmon strips and coffee along the road.

"Nowadays they got air support. The first guys going through, they're the elite. The guys in the back who are not making good time, they're the ones you want to help."

EAGLE ISLAND

POPULATION: 0

MILES FROM GRAYLING: 60

▲ Above: Ralph Canatser, an Eagle Island perennial.
▶ A hand-painted sign welcomes mushers to "The Jewel of the Yukon."

The Canatser family jumped onto the Iditarod bandwagon in 1977, the first year the race followed the southern route. Ralph, Helmi, and their son, Steve, were then living in a twelve-by-fourteen-foot cabin along a slough of the Yukon River. Steve, who was home-schooled by his mother, remembers those early years as somewhat primitive. Life became easier when the family purchased a generator and built a second cabin. And the

Iditarod was a welcome break after a winter without seeing a soul.

"In the spring about March the planes would bring in the food, and the officials would come through, and then here came all the mushers," Steve says. "Then when it was all over, it seemed like the river was breaking up. It kind of made the long winters shorter.

"I think what made the place was Mom. She was just an extraordinary woman. No one was favored. We never had any water facilities, but come to feeding people, or getting hot water for their thermoses, she gave it all to the mushers—even the officials.

"She always made cheesecake for Rick Swenson. One year Swenson left behind some of the cream cheese that he was feeding to his dogs. The next time he came through Mom had made cheesecake for him. Everybody loved it. And Rick always joked that he had to be first there to get a piece of cheesecake."

Helmi has been sorely missed since her death in 1992. Of the family's two cabins, the newer one burned in 1994, but the original still shelters Ralph and Steve when they come to commercial fish in the summer. At seventy, Steve says, his father is "as ornery as ever."

From Eagle Island, the trail follows the Yukon River to Kaltag, the last of the Athabascan villages, where the northern and southern routes rejoin. Departing from Kaltag, mushers leave Interior Alaska, cross the Nulato Hills, and enter Eskimo country, where the treeless regions of the Bering Sea coast offer new challenges.

▼ Hawaii resident Pat Likos bundles up for a long wait in the cold. She met her husband Tommy years ago, when both were volunteering for the Iditarod. A week together on Eagle Island and they fell in love.

UNALAKLEET

(YOU-*na-la-kleet*)

POPULATION: 798

MILES FROM KALTAG: 90

◄◄ **Unalakleet is a place of drifting snow and storms.**

▲ **Locals turn out in numbers to greet the racers.**

▶ **Jeff King shares a bed of straw with his team.**

The Gold Coast Award, a trophy and $2,500 in gold nuggets, is waiting for the first musher to Unalakleet, the largest community between Wasilla and Nome. Here along the coast, sudden storms off the Bering Sea can be brutal. But according to Race Manager Jack Niggemyer, this village offers a warm welcome.

"To me, the best reception in any village at all is in Unalakleet. They let kids out of school, and the entire town comes out to watch. They're crowding around like maggots on a gut pile."

Unalakleet is an Inupiat Eskimo word meaning "where the east wind blows," and blow it does. Drifting snow can reach the rooftops. This is one of the few checkpoints on the trail where mushers change sleds, exchanging their freighting sleds for lighter-weight racing sleds. It's the last of the soft snow; from here out, the landscape is windblown.

This is where the race turns into a true endurance test because of the weather, according to lifelong resident Sam Towarak.

"It's evolved that way," he says. "The elements change when they leave the calm of the Interior, and they hit the wind."

So many Unalakleet residents are anxious to see the incoming racers that they travel several miles out of town to a BLM shelter cabin called Old Woman Cabin, where they can meet the front-runners even before they reach the city limits.

"Real familiar to the mushers is the Old Woman Cabin," Towarak says. "Stories abound because of the many varied spirits that live on that part of the road. Those guys are real tired, plus it's an eerie part of the trip, one of the more quiet places. The northern lights are happening and the little spirits. . . . When the mushers come down the trail, it's usually moonlight or it's bright, the stars light it, there's always an eerie feeling about that area. There's stories there."

SHAKTOOLIK

(*shak*-TOO-*lick*)

POPULATION: 231

MILES FROM UNALAKLEET: 40

▲ Tom Dotomain of Shaktoolik peers down the trail in search of incoming mushers.

▶ Charlie Boulding waves to a fan as he glides down the main street of Shaktoolik, which lies on the Bering Sea coast.

Although there are five more checkpoints before Nome, the villagers of Shaktoolik can often predict who'll get there first.

"We look at the way their dogs look and the way the mushers look, and we pretty much know who's going to cross the finish line first," says Palmer Sagoonick, a reindeer herder who eagerly awaits the Iditarod each year. When the mushers come through, he hits them with questions. That's because Palmer (and he says to remember that name) is an Iditarod musher in the making.

"For me, they're an encyclopedia of dog mushing. I bombard mushers with questions. They give me a lot of information. Some are tired and won't talk."

Palmer started his own recreational team in 1994. He read and highlighted every mushing book he could find, including one by former Iditarod champion Joe Runyan. He wanted a competitive team, but couldn't afford dogs from top bloodlines. So one year he posted a sign at the checkpoint. It read: "Wanted: Sick, tired, old, retired Iditarod dogs. I'll give them a good home and plenty of exercise."

A few weeks after the race, he got a call from Iditarod headquarters. Did he want fourteen sick, tired, old Iditarod dogs?

"Out of the fourteen, I have only two left—because they were that old. But I have their puppies. I have a real competitive team now and I've been running mid-distance."

When he's not working with his dogs, Palmer is a reindeer herder with a grazing permit of .75 million acres of open range. The only fence is around his corral—he rounds up the deer for health checks and vaccines.

"The caribou migration has really gone through my range. Over the last ten years I lost half my herd. I had over two thousand. Half met up with their brothers and marched off. Not much you can do."

In the meantime, Palmer Sagoonick trains for the Iditarod. "I'll run when I'm ready and when I'm competitive," he says. And if he should win some day?

"Now that would be a Cinderella story."

KOYUK

(COY-*uck*)

POPULATION: 280

MILES FROM SHAKTOOLIK: 58

▲ Packing along a baby, a Koyuk woman fishes through the ice.

▶ With plenty of spectators and press standing by, Martin Buser tends to his resting dog team.

Like other Native communities along the Iditarod, Koyuk is a village that mixes reliance on fish and game with a cash economy.

"I think Koyuk is famous for subsistence," says Raymond Douglas, who's lived here all his life. "All through the year, we have different seasons of subsistence. In the springtime: birds, and fish through the ice. In June we have fish, all kinds, and we fish until July. Fall, we are looking for beluga whales, moose, caribou. In the month of October we'll be looking for fish again, tomcods and mudfish, and caribou. After freezeup, trapping will be going on and caribou hunting."

At the head of Norton Sound, Koyuk is the northernmost checkpoint at just shy of sixty-five degrees north. From Shaktoolik, mushers cross the frozen sea ice on a trail that's all but invisible during storms. Orange-topped trail markers and surveyor's flagging are all that guide the racers.

Raymond, who's been a checker since 1974, remembers blowing snow and stormy weather as the norm rather than the exception.

"Used to be kind of tough when they'd come all at once, two or three in the morning, when the temperature's kind of cold. It stays about thirty-five below about that time."

The checkpoint varies—some years it's in the community building, or at the game hall, in the old medical building, or in the armory. Recently it was in a local man's home. Regardless of the checkpoint location, Raymond's routine is still the same.

"In the early part, I get a letter from race headquarters telling me who's going to be in the race, how many bags of dog food they've got. Then I'd be looking for them." Like volunteers elsewhere, he meets planes, hauls food, checks in mushers, and does the mop-up work. Lately, however, Raymond has been grateful for the addition of volunteers imported from around the United States.

"Last year I did real good on sleep 'cause I had real good helpers."

ELIM
(EE-*lum*)

POPULATION: 284

MILES FROM KOYUK: 48

▼ **Riding in a sled towed behind a snowmachine, local children are taken to see the mushers.**

City Manager Luther Nagaruk is matter-of-fact about the dangers of mushing along the Bering Sea coast. Around Elim, however, guides watch out for travelers on the wind-swept trail.

"During some storms, mushers get lost," Luther says. "What we usually do is—and this is all voluntary by local people—if it's storming and if somebody gets lost, these guys will go out there and find them and get them back on the trail.

"The one time Joe Garnie got lost, he was out in a different direction in a blizzard. When they found him, he was buried under the snow. They got him back on the trail. The people here know the area real well. They can usually find somebody out there in a blizzard."

Luther also speaks of another kind of guardian that's as puzzling as the stories from around Old Woman Cabin.

"We have some ghosts between here and Koyuk," he says. "These are lights. Usually if you're going too far out on the ice, these lights come on along the coast. I've seen it myself. The Iditarod dog mushers have seen them, too. Mostly near the old settlements along the coast.

"Strange things happen. Never to hurt anybody; mostly to help people. I know one musher that was coming by here one time. He stopped against a fence, he thought it was a graveyard. He camped there and when he woke up the next morning, there was no fence there."

From Elim, mushers continue along the coastline, then travel west through the hills to Golovin.

GOLOVIN

(GOL-*uh-vin*)

POPULATION: 161

MILES FROM ELIM: 28

▲ **Dick Mackey has entered the Iditarod eight times.**

▼ **Rick Swenson passes through Golovin.**

Golovin was founded on a point between Golovnin Bay and Golovnin Lagoon. So why was the village name spelled without the extra "n"? It seems to be a typo that stuck. The bay was named in 1821 by a member of the Imperial Russian Navy for his vessel, which had been named for another navy man, Captain Vasili Mikhailovich Golovnin. When gold was discovered to the north in 1898, a trading post here gained prominence as a supply center, and a town grew in this place. Somewhere along the way, the "n" was dropped in the bay and lagoon names, too.

Iditarod champion Dick Mackey remembers coming into Golovin during the first running of the race in 1973:

"At that time everyone stayed in someone's home. In the early days people vied for the privilege of you coming to their homes. I came in after dark and was sent to the Martin Olson residence. Maggie Olson came to the door and invited me into the living room. There was just a faint light on in another part of the house. I sat down, I'm just beat, and assumed that I was all alone in the dark. Maggie had gone upstairs to get her husband. Then, right by my right ear, this voice says, 'HELLO!' I just about . . . Turns out it was a bird that they had let loose to fly around in their house.

"The next morning I came out and started off with my team. I've got one dog that looked like a hog, all bloated up. And it started throwing up. I thought, 'What on earth?' I set the hook and went up and felt the dog—it was actually sloshing in its stomach. We kept going and it kept vomiting every so often, and seemed to get better. Later on when I saw Martin again, he said, 'You've got some pretty good dogs there. Your dogs ate five gallons of seal oil.'

"It was that one dog. If he hadn't thrown it up, it would have killed him for sure."

WHITE MOUNTAIN

POPULATION: 212

MILES FROM GOLOVIN: 18

▼ **Nearing the end of the race, Jeff King's dogs take a break for a snow bath and a stretch.**

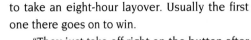

Golovin is treeless and yet eighteen miles later at White Mountain, mushers are temporarily back in the trees and protected from the wind.

"We have two hills," says lifelong resident Howard Lincoln. "One on the north side and one on the east side. The only time we have wind is when it's from the south. If you see the village from Golovin, from a distance, the white rocks are up there, and that's why they call it White Mountain."

At this checkpoint, mushers are required to take an eight-hour layover. Usually the first one there goes on to win.

"They just take off right on the button after they take their eight hours," says Howard, who's been checking for so long that he's lost track of the years. "They don't even wait a minute. The first twenty teams, they get some money.

"I give weather reports to Nome in the morning, and in the afternoon again around three until the Red Lantern person [last finisher] comes through. After he leaves, then I stop giving weather to Nome.

"One or two times the Red Lantern had to come back on account of their dogs, a couple miles up the river; like a flat tire on a car or a truck, they just lay down and they don't want to go anymore. The mushers turn them around and they come back real quick. It happened to Norman Vaughan's wife—they were courting that year. The dogs quit. She turned the team around and they came back. The next morning, I went out on a snowmachine ahead of the dogs about five or six miles out of the village, then she waved me to get off the trail so they could go by. She was the Red Lantern. There's always something happening like that."

SAFETY

POPULATION: 0

MILES FROM WHITE

MOUNTAIN: 55

Mushers follow the shore of Norton Sound to Safety, where the checkpoint building provides the only light for miles.

"To me, it just looks like an old shack, but in winter, it's like a lighthouse," remembers DeeDee Jonrowe. "It always looks like a lantern in the distance. You can probably see it four or five miles away."

According to former Nome mayor Leo Rasmussen, the present checkpoint building had a previous life in Nome, where in the late 1930s it was a motion picture theater known as the "Nomerama." A half-century later, it was cut into sections and rebuilt at Safety.

The place was so named because of its natural harbor, known for protecting ships. From Safety, mushers must wear their numbered bibs for the final leg of the journey.

◀ The colors of land and sea blur together this time of year. Mushers like Martin Buser, shown here, must be careful to follow official Iditarod Trail markers.

▶ The "Nomerama" is a welcome sight among mushers who are approaching the last leg of the grueling race.

7   THE END OF THE TRAIL

NOME

POPULATION: 3,511

MILES FROM SAFETY: 22

◄◄ Shawn Sidelinger passes by Farley's Camp, a small settlement just outside Nome.

▲ Three-time champion Martin Buser poses with his leaders, Blondie and Fearless, at the 1997 awards banquet in Nome.

► A flurry of fans, media, and Iditarod officials await Wayne Curtis as he approaches the finish line under the burl arch.

As the first-place musher nears town, Nome comes to life, reawakening the excitement of its riotous gold rush past. Everybody's invited to join the frenzy on Front Street. Spectators line the street, flush with celebratory spirits and biting cold. The burl wood archway marking the finish line is in place. A platform stands ready to host post-race interviews and picture-taking sessions of the champion and the leaders draped in yellow roses. Dozens of press photographers and television cameramen wait to capture the winning moment.

The prize for finishing first: $50,000 and a four-wheel drive truck. The remaining $350,000 in the purse is distributed among the mushers taking up to twentieth place. Those finishing from twenty-first place to last place can receive up to $1,049 from money generated by the

Idita-Rider program (a fund-raiser in which fans bid for the privilege of riding in a musher's sled during the first stretch of the race from Anchorage to Eagle River). At the mushers' banquet on the following Sunday, a host of other awards are distributed, from drawings for cash to recognition of sportsmanship and excellence in dog care.

KNOM radio reporter Tom Busch, who's provided live coverage of the finish for twenty years, remembers how in 1993 blowing snow knocked out visibility as four confused rookie mushers approached town.

"They didn't know where the trail was. They were kind of wandering around town looking for the finish line. We got calls that there were Iditarod mushers at the other end of town. And there was nobody at the line, except for Jim Brown, the photographer, when this musher Paul Rupple was finally coming down Front Street—the wrong way.

"If Jim hadn't helped the guy, he would have been the only one to finish the Iditarod going backwards."

Nome residents Howard and Julie Farley and former Mayor of Nome Leo Rasmussen were key people in launching the Iditarod Trail Sled Dog Race more than twenty-five years ago and have supported it ever since. Rasmussen made it a point to be at the finish line to shake the hand of every musher who crossed the line, first to last. He has missed only a few competitors over the years.

"They're really gracious hosts to allow us to come in and create chaos in their community," says Race Manager Jack Niggemyer, who by the race's end has relocated his headquarters to Nome's mini-convention center. With the arrival of the first-place finisher, the race is far from over.

"There's people in there twenty-four hours a day," Niggemyer says. "We're tracking people on the phones and stuff. But there are other little functions going on. And we have a big musher autograph party at some point. It's real lively."

Nome stays on alert until the last of the mushers appears to pick up the Red Lantern Award. A team of Niggemyer's "trail sweeps" arrives with garbage bags full of dog booties and other debris they've picked up along the trail. Then a thousand volunteers will go back to their normal lives in Alaska and across the United States, and a new champion will represent Alaska's favorite sport for another year.

▲ "Father of the Iditarod" Joe Redington Sr. is honored at the Nome awards banquet in 1997, the twenty-fifth anniversary of the race he founded. He finished the race that year at age eighty.
▶▶ David Olesen prepares a meal for his tired dogs. In the foreground is his leader, named Tamarack the Maniac.